ALL JAZZED UP!
INTERMEDIATE PIANO SOLO

ISBN 978-1-4950-4517-2

Wonderland Music Company, Inc.
Walt Disney Music Company

DISTRIBUTED BY

7777 W. BLUEMOUND RD. P.O. BOX 13819 MILWAUKEE, WI 53213

In Australia Contact:
Hal Leonard Australia Pty. Ltd.
4 Lentara Court
Cheltenham, Victoria, 3192 Australia
Email: ausadmin@halleonard.com.au

Visit Hal Leonard Online at
www.halleonard.com

BELLE

from Walt Disney's BEAUTY AND THE BEAST

Music by ALAN MENKEN
Lyrics by HOWARD ASHMAN

Rather fast, straight 8ths

sim.

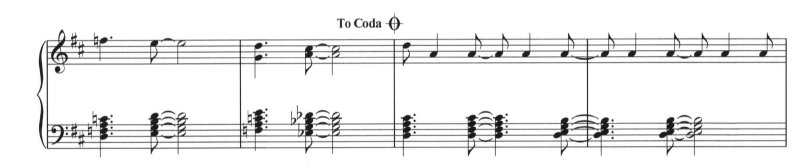

To Coda ⊕

Swing(♩♪ = ♪³♪)

D.S. al Coda
(take 2nd ending)

CODA

rit.

CIRCLE OF LIFE
from Walt Disney Pictures' THE LION KING

Music by ELTON JOHN
Lyrics by TIM RICE

Moderately slow

CRUELLA DE VIL
from Walt Disney's 101 DALMATIONS

Words and Music by
MEL LEVEN

EV'RYBODY WANTS TO BE A CAT

from Walt Disney's THE ARISTOCATS

Words by FLOYD HUDDLESTON
Music by AL RINKER

Moderately

IT'S A SMALL WORLD

from Disneyland Resort® and Magic Kingdom® Park

Words and Music by RICHARD M. SHERMAN
and ROBERT B. SHERMAN

Boogie Woogie, straight 8ths

Swing

LET IT GO
from Disney's Animated Feature FROZEN

Music and Lyrics by KRISTEN ANDERSON-LOPEZ
and ROBERT LOPEZ

Moderate Swing

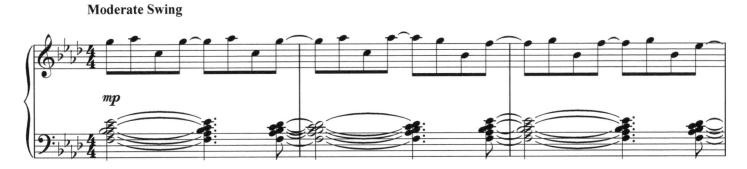

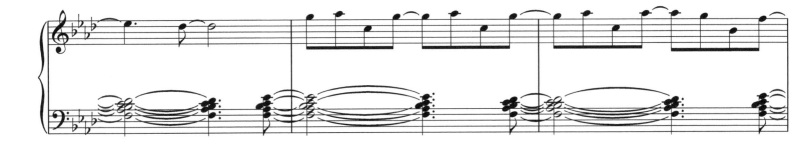

Straight 8ths

To Coda ⊕
Straight 8ths

Swing

Straight 8ths

D.S. al Coda

Swing

CODA **Straight 8ths**

N.C.

f

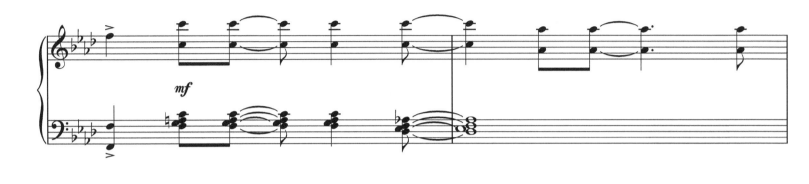

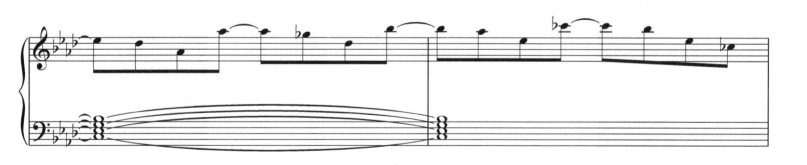

MICKEY MOUSE MARCH

from Walt Disney's THE MICKEY MOUSE CLUB

Words and Music by
JIMMIE DODD

Moderately fast

ONCE UPON A DREAM
from Walt Disney's SLEEPING BEAUTY

Words and Music by SAMMY FAIN and JACK LAWRENCE
Adapted from a Theme by TCHAIKOVSKY

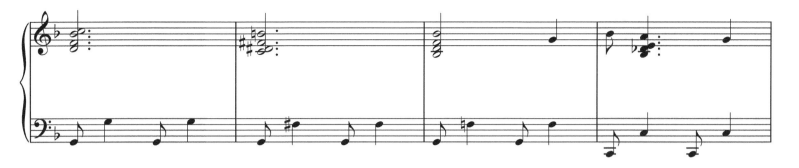

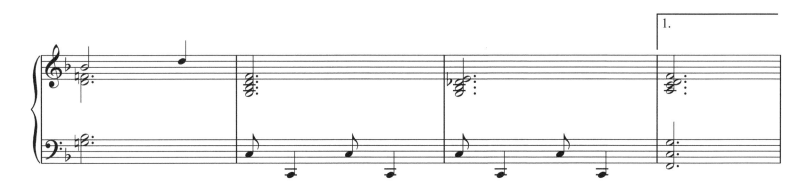

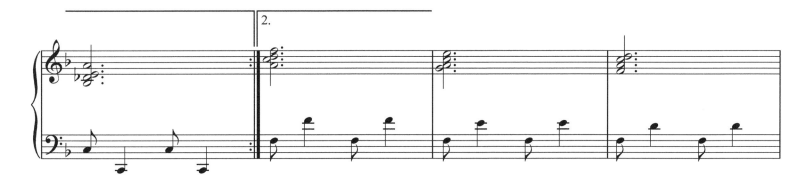

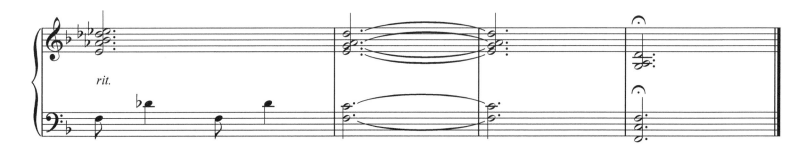

SUPERCALIFRAGILISTICEXPIALIDOCIOUS

from Walt Disney's MARY POPPINS

Words and Music by RICHARD M. SHERMAN
and ROBERT B. SHERMAN

Moderately fast Latin

PART OF YOUR WORLD

from Walt Disney's THE LITTLE MERMAID

Music by ALAN MENKEN
Lyrics by HOWARD ASHMAN

Moderately fast

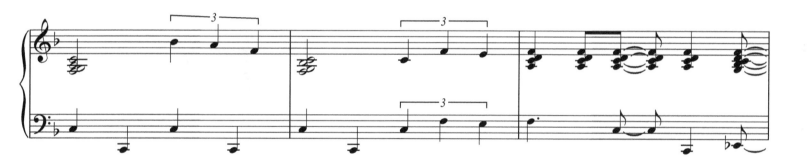

UNDER THE SEA
from Walt Disney's THE LITTLE MERMAID

Music by ALAN MENKEN
Lyrics by HOWARD ASHMAN

In a driving dance beat

WHEN SHE LOVED ME

from Walt Disney Pictures' TOY STORY 2 - A Pixar Film

Music and Lyrics by
RANDY NEWMAN

Tenderly, very freely

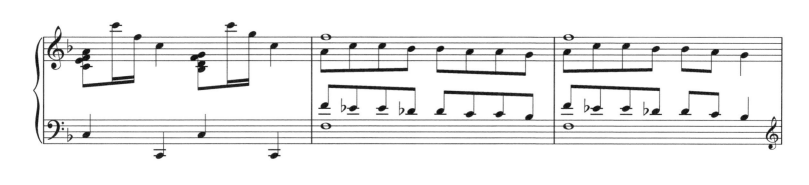

ALL JAZZED UP!

FROM HAL LEONARD

In this series, popular favorites receive unexpected fresh treatments. Uniquely reimagined and crafted for intermediate piano solo, these tunes have been All Jazzed Up!

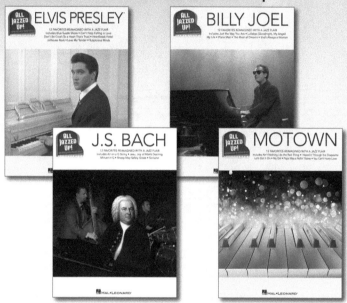

J.S. BACH
Air on the G String • Aria • Bist du bei mir (Be Thou with Me) • Gavotte • Jesu, Joy of Man's Desiring • Largo • March • Minuet in G • Musette • Sheep May Safely Graze • Siciliano • Sleepers, Awake (Wachet Auf).
00151064..$12.99

THE BEATLES
All My Loving • And I Love Her • Come Together • Eight Days a Week • Eleanor Rigby • The Fool on the Hill • Here, There and Everywhere • Lady Madonna • Lucy in the Sky with Diamonds • Michelle • While My Guitar Gently Weeps • Yesterday.
00172235..$12.99

CHRISTMAS CAROLS
Auld Lang Syne • Deck the Hall • The First Noel • Good King Wenceslas • In the Bleak Midwinter • Jingle Bells • Joy to the World • O Christmas Tree • O Come, All Ye Faithful • O Little Town of Bethlehem • Up on the Housetop • We Wish You a Merry Christmas.
00277866..$12.99

CHRISTMAS SONGS
Blue Christmas • The Christmas Song (Chestnuts Roasting on an Open Fire) • Christmas Time Is Here • Do You Hear What I Hear • Feliz Navidad • Have Yourself a Merry Little Christmas • I'll Be Home for Christmas • Merry Christmas, Darling • Silver Bells • Sleigh Ride • White Christmas • Winter Wonderland.
00236706..$12.99

COLDPLAY
Clocks • Don't Panic • Every Teardrop Is a Waterfall • Fix You • Magic • Paradise • The Scientist • A Sky Full of Stars • Speed of Sound • Trouble • Viva La Vida • Yellow.
00149026..$12.99

DISNEY
Belle • Circle of Life • Cruella De Vil • Ev'rybody Wants to Be a Cat • It's a Small World • Let It Go • Mickey Mouse March • Once upon a Dream • Part of Your World • Supercalifragilisticexpialidocious • Under the Sea • When She Loved Me.
00151072..$14.99

JIMI HENDRIX
Castles Made of Sand • Crosstown Traffic • Fire • Foxey Lady • Hey Joe • Little Wing • Manic Depression • Purple Haze • Spanish Castle Magic • The Wind Cries Mary.
00174441..$12.99

BILLY JOEL
And So It Goes • Honesty • It's Still Rock and Roll to Me • Just the Way You Are • The Longest Time • Lullabye (Goodnight, My Angel) • My Life • New York State of Mind • Piano Man • The River of Dreams • She's Always a Woman • She's Got a Way.
00149039..$12.99

MOTOWN
Ain't Nothing like the Real Thing • How Sweet It Is (To Be Loved by You) • I Can't Help Myself (Sugar Pie, Honey Bunch) • I Heard It Through the Grapevine • I Want You Back • Let's Get It On • My Girl • Never Can Say Goodbye • Overjoyed • Papa Was a Rollin' Stone • Still • You Can't Hurry Love.
00174482..$12.99

NIRVANA
About a Girl • All Apologies • Come as You Are • Dumb • Heart Shaped Box • In Bloom • Lithium • The Man Who Sold the World • On a Plain • (New Wave) Polly • Rape Me • Smells like Teen Spirit.
00149025..$12.99

OZZY OSBOURNE
Crazy Train • Dreamer • Flying High Again • Goodbye to Romance • Iron Man • Mama, I'm Coming Home • Mr. Crowley • No More Tears • Over the Mountain • Paranoid • Perry Mason • Time After Time.
00149040..$12.99

ELVIS PRESLEY
Blue Suede Shoes • Can't Help Falling in Love • Cryin' in the Chapel • Don't • Don't Be Cruel (To a Heart That's True) • Heartbreak Hotel • I Want You, I Need You, I Love You • Jailhouse Rock • Love Me Tender • Suspicious Minds • The Wonder of You • You Don't Have to Say You Love Me.
00198895..$12.99

STEVIE WONDER
As • Ebony and Ivory • For Once in My Life • I Just Called to Say I Love You • I Wish • Isn't She Lovely • My Cherie Amour • Ribbon in the Sky • Signed, Sealed, Delivered I'm Yours • Sir Duke • Superstition • You Are the Sunshine of My Life.
00149090..$12.99

HAL•LEONARD®
www.halleonard.com

Prices, contents and availability subject to change without notice.

Disney characters and artwork © Disney Enterprises, Inc.

0618